A Guide to the
Manhattan Project
in
New Mexico

Cynthia C. Kelly
President, Atomic Heritage Foundation

Introduced by Richard Rhodes

Introduction

In 1942, when the physicist J. Robert Oppenheimer was recruiting scientists for the U.S. atomic bomb program, secrecy prevented him from revealing to them what their work would be. He told them instead that the outcome, if successful, would probably end the war and might, he said, end all war.

The atomic bomb did contribute to ending the Pacific War, and fear of its destructiveness has limited major war now for more than sixty-five years. What began as a desperate effort of defense—invent an atomic bomb before Nazi Germany got there first—became a major new force in human affairs.

The work of physics, chemistry, metallurgy and engineering that led to the new invention was accomplished in requisitioned or makeshift buildings, laboratories and factories all over the United States. No state contributed more directly to the vast project than New Mexico. The state was home to the secret laboratory, Los Alamos, high and secure on the Pajarito plateau, where the new weapon was designed and assembled.

New Mexico also provided the site where the more complicated of the two types of bombs Los Alamos invented was tested—Trinity Site, near Alamogordo, the first place to bear the scars of an atomic explosion. Scientists came here from Europe, England and elsewhere in the United States to live and work, an effort shared by Army enlistees, New Mexican citizens, Native Americans and a few Soviet spies. From the Paleolithic era to the Atomic Age, few other regions bear such an interesting, hopeful—and picturesque!—freight of history.

Richard Rhodes

Richard Rhodes, author, *The Making of the Atomic Bomb*

Table of Contents

Welcome	5
Atomic Basics	6
Center of the Universe	8
The Race for the Bomb	12

EN ROUTE TO LOS ALAMOS — 17
- Arriving in New Mexico — 18
- 109 East Palace — 20
- La Fonda — 22
- Castillo Street Bridge — 23
- The Pueblos — 24
- Otowi Bridge — 26

LOS ALAMOS — 29
- P.O. Box 1663 — 30
- Fuller Lodge — 31
- Bathtub Row — 32
- Oppenheimer House — 34
- Los Alamos the Boomtown — 36
- Perro Caliente — 37
- The V-Site — 38
- The Gun Site — 40
- The Concrete Bowl — 42
- Quonset Hut — 43
- Louis Slotin Building — 44
- Pond Cabin — 45

THE TRINITY SITE — 47
- McDonald Ranch House — 48
- Ground Zero — 50
- Trinity Site — 53
- Hilton Hotel — 55

Sources	58
Chronology	60
Places to See	63
Maps	64

J. Robert Oppenheimer and General Leslie R. Groves at the Trinity test site
Photo courtesy of the U.S. Department of Energy

Welcome
ATOMIC HERITAGE FOUNDATION

The Land of Enchantment was a crucible for the world's first atomic bomb during World War II. This guidebook combines the expertise and resources of the Atomic Heritage Foundation and leading Manhattan Project authorities to bring you history, science, personal accounts and insights into New Mexico's past.

At the time of publication, we are hopeful that Congress will soon pass legislation creating a Manhattan Project National Historical Park at Los Alamos, NM, as well as at the production sites of Oak Ridge, TN, and Hanford, WA. Eventually, other Manhattan Project sites such as the Trinity Site and Wendover Airfield may become associated areas.

The guidebook invites you to visit the train station at Lamy where bewildered recruits arrived not knowing where they were or where they were going. Visitors to 109 East Palace in Santa Fe can see where the Manhattan Project's gatekeeper, Dorothy McKibbin, secretly provided valuable reassurance and practical advice to the newcomers.

Travel to the Pajarito Plateau and see the former "secret city" of Los Alamos, the Bathtub Row houses, where the world's top physicists lived, and Fuller Lodge, the social center of the Manhattan Project. Check out the places in Santa Fe where Soviet spies met their Manhattan Project contacts. Learn about the histories of the Pueblos and Hispanic communities and how they were affected by the Manhattan Project. See where the nuclear age began at the Trinity Site.

Not all of the Manhattan Project properties mentioned here are restored or accessible to the public. We expect this will change as a Manhattan Project National Historical Park is established. In the meantime, there are plenty of sites to see and excellent museums to visit. Enjoy your trip!

Cynthia C. Kelly

Cynthia C. Kelly
President

Atomic Basics
THE SCIENCE BEHIND THE BOMB

Everything around us is made of **atoms**. Atoms are the smallest units that make up **elements**. At the heart of the atom is the **nucleus**, which is made up of two kinds of subatomic particles: **protons**, with a positive electric charge, and **neutrons**, with no charge. **Electrons**, with a negative charge, orbit around the nucleus. The nucleus is bound together by an incredibly strong energetic force. When the nucleus splits, nuclear energy is released.

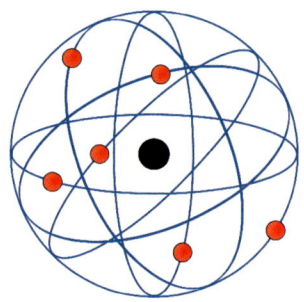

Photo courtesy of Colin M. Burtnett, Wikimedia Commons

Isotopes are different forms of the same element. They have the same number of protons and electrons but a different number of neutrons. Two naturally-occurring isotopes of uranium are **uranium-235** with 143 neutrons (235 heavy particles) and **uranium-238** with 146 neutrons (238 heavy particles).

Those extra three neutrons make all the difference. U-235 is much more unstable than U-238 and easily splits apart ("fissions") when hit by another neutron.

> **NUCLEAR TERMINOLOGY**
> **Atom:** building block of matter; made up of a small, dense nucleus surrounded by a cloud of negatively-charged **electrons.**
> **Nucleus:** makes up the center of the atom; consists of a number of positively-charged **protons** and neutral **neutrons**. An atom is classified by the number of protons and neutrons in its nucleus.
> **Isotope:** Isotopes of an element possess the same number of protons in their nuclei but have different numbers of neutrons.
> **Fission:** the process by which an atom's nucleus is split into smaller pieces; results in the release of neutrons and lots of energy.
> **Pile:** a nuclear reactor. Coined by Enrico Fermi at the Met Lab, it was based on the first rudimentary nuclear reactor, which was nothing more than a pile of uranium and graphite blocks.

The atoms of most elements—like hydrogen, oxygen, iron, or lead—are stable. Their nuclei tend to stay together rather than break apart. But uranium-235 is different. When a nucleus of this isotope is hit by a speeding neutron, it **fissions**, or splits, into two smaller nuclei plus one to three extra neutrons—and releases a lot of energy. The extra neutrons smash into more nuclei, fissioning them and releasing even more neutrons in a cascade of incredible energy.

This is called a **nuclear chain reaction.** When controlled inside a reactor, a chain reaction can use a small amount of U-235 or plutonium fuel to generate massive amounts of energy.

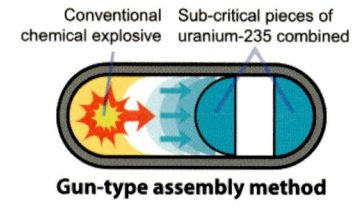
Gun-type assembly method

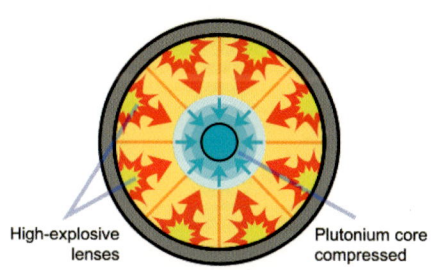
Implosion assembly method

Image courtesy of Wikimedia Commons

FAT MAN AND LITTLE BOY
In order to detonate a nuclear weapon, you need a **critical mass** of fissionable material to ensure that the neutrons released by fission will strike another nucleus and release its neutrons, producing a chain reaction. The more fissionable material you have, the greater the odds that such an event will occur.

The U.S. developed two types of atomic bombs during the Second World War using different fissionable materials--enriched uranium (U-235) and plutonium (Pu-239). Each bomb was designed to bring subcritical masses together to produce a critical mass. "**Little Boy**," dropped on Hiroshima, was a gun-type weapon with an enriched uranium core. "**Fat Man**," dropped on Nagasaki, was an implosion-type device with a plutonium core.

Center of the Universe
PAJARITO PLATEAU

The ancient Ancestral Pueblo people considered the Pajarito Plateau the center of the universe. To the east are the majestic Sangre de Cristo Mountains, the southern part of the Rocky Mountains, and to the west, the Jemez Mountains.

At 7,300 feet above sea level, the Pajarito (Spanish for "Little Bird") Plateau provides stunning views high above the Rio Grande. The Plateau was home to the Ancestral Puebloan culture more than eight centuries ago.

GEOLOGY
The Pajarito Plateau is primarily composed of orange-pink rock or ignimbrite. The rock was formed when the nearby Valles Caldera volcano erupted over one million years ago. With an average of 14 inches of rain a year, it is an ecologically fragile high desert.

The Ancestral Puebloan civilization began in 1200 BC in the Four Corners area and eventually extended to large parts of Arizona, Utah, Colorado and New Mexico. From 850 AD, Chaco Canyon, now a National Historical Park and World Heritage Site, was the hub of ceremony and trade for the prehistoric Four Corners area for 400 years.

The Ancestral Pueblo people settled along the Rio Grande and on the Pajarito Plateau between the years 1175 and 1250 AD, building homes along canyon walls and farming beans, corn and squash on the mesa tops. Visitors can see the remains of their dwellings and artifacts in what is now Bandelier National Monument.

A cliff face at Bandelier National Monument
Photo courtesy of Andrew Dunn, Wikimedia Commons

Archaeologists believe that droughts and intertribal warfare forced the inhabitants of the Pajarito Plateau to leave for more fertile ground near the Rio Grande. By 1550, they had abandoned the plateau. Among the descendants of the Ancestral Pueblo people are the eight Indian Pueblos in northern New Mexico, including the San Ildefonso, Ohkay Owingeh, Santa Clara, Pojoaque, Tesuque, Nambé, Picuris and Taos, as well as the Cochiti and the Jemez Pueblos.

In the sixteenth century, the Spanish brought horses, guns and the Catholic religion up from Mexico. The Province of New Mexico (now New Mexico and Arizona) became part of New Spain. Santa Fe was declared the capital in 1610 and has remained an important center of government, trade and culture for more than four centuries.

Descendants of the early Spanish settlers began settling the Pajarito Plateau in the nineteenth century. Beginning in 1821, the Santa Fe Trail brought thousands of people to northern New Mexico. The incorporation of the Territory of New Mexico into the United States in 1848 spurred further development. In 1878, the Santa Fe Railway reached New Mexico. In 1912, New Mexico became the forty-seventh state, with a population of 327,000.

Under the Homestead Act, U.S. citizens could claim 160 acres of land in exchange for living there for five years. Homesteaders Victor and Refugio Romero and their six children built a cabin on the Pajarito Plateau in 1913. The recently restored cabin is one of two remaining from the homesteading era on the Pajarito Plateau.

Romero Cabin
Photo courtesy of the Los Alamos Historical Museum Archives

In the early 1920s, New Mexico became a haven for "health seekers." The altitude, air quality, plentiful sunshine and mild climate seemed to promote recovery of all kinds of health troubles. Many artists and writers who came to New Mexico for health reasons never left.

J. Robert Oppenheimer was one of the health seekers. In 1922, his parents arranged for the 18-year-old to spend the summer in New

Mexico to recover his strength after a near-fatal case of dysentery. Robert stayed at a dude ranch 25 miles northeast of Santa Fe with high school teacher Herbert Smith as a companion and mentor. From there, he took five- or six-day horseback trips through the surrounding wilderness, camping out in the rugged mountains. This experience restored Oppenheimer's health and instilled a deep love for the desert high country. He returned to northern New Mexico repeatedly, bringing his brother Frank and many friends.

By 1942, Oppenheimer was one of the world's leading theoretical physicists at the University of California, Berkeley. When he was appointed scientific director of a top-secret weapons project, he suggested the Los Alamos Ranch School as an ideal site for the laboratory. In early 1943, the school turned over its 800 acres to the secret project. The Pajarito Plateau soon became the center of an effort that would harness the energy of the atom. For Oppenheimer, it was a marriage of his two great loves, physics and New Mexico.

LOS ALAMOS RANCH SCHOOL
In 1918, entrepreneur Ashley Pond began an "outdoor school" at Los Alamos to provide boys a chance to gain health, strength and self-confidence. The Los Alamos Ranch School combined a rigorous outdoor experience with a college preparatory education.

Los Alamos Ranch School's Fuller Lodge
Photo courtesy of the Los Alamos Historical Museum Archives

The Race for the Bomb

In a letter dated August 2, 1939, Albert Einstein warned President Franklin D. Roosevelt that Germany was probably working to produce an "extremely powerful" bomb. Einstein hoped to galvanize the United States into developing an atomic bomb before Hitler did.

Albert Einstein meets with Leo Szilard to compose his letter to FDR
Photo courtesy of the U.S. Department of Energy

In response to Einstein's letter and the urging of British prime minister Winston Churchill, President Roosevelt authorized a top-secret effort to build an atomic bomb. Organized as a military effort under the Army Corps of Engineers, scientists were recruited to work on the project from the leading universities and laboratories across the United States. In addition, scientists from Great Britain and Canada came as part of the British Mission led by Sir James Chadwick, who was awarded the Nobel Prize for his 1932 discovery of the neutron.

Dozens of refugees from Europe, many of them also Nobel Prize-winning scientists, joined the project. Together, physicists, chemists, engineers, mathematicians and other scientists designed, built and tested the world's first atomic bombs. Their drive to uncover nature's innermost secrets was combined with a sense of patriotic duty to contribute to the war effort.

Lise Meitner & Otto Hahn
Photo courtesy of the U.S. Department of Energy

LISE MEITNER: REFUGEE FROM THE NAZIS
Being Jewish, Lise Meitner was subject to the increasingly repressive anti-Semitic laws. Because so many Jewish intellectuals had already fled, in July 1938 German authorities forbade academics to emigrate. Leaving Berlin by train, Meitner barely escaped when Nazi officials inspected her expired Austrian passport at the Holland border. She continued her study of uranium atoms in exile in Sweden. Though slim and shy, Lise was a formidable physicist and found in her work an escape from her loneliness in exile.

Research related to an atomic bomb began long before World War II. As early as 1933, Hungarian Leo Szilard conceived of the possibility of a chain reaction, the explosive force that powers an atomic bomb. In 1934, Italian physicist Enrico Fermi turned up further evidence that atomic fission, or splitting the nucleus of the atom in multiple fragments and starting a chain reaction, was possible. The question was, which element had a nucleus that could be split easily?

At the Kaiser Wilhelm Institute in Berlin, Austrian physicist Lise Meitner and German chemists Otto Hahn and Fritz Strassmann studied Fermi's data. By accident, the German chemists discovered that uranium atoms bombarded by neutrons broke into lighter particles. Otto Hahn was so disturbed by the possible military implications of his discovery that he contemplated suicide.

In December 1938, Lise Meitner correctly read the Hahn-Strassmann experiments as evidence that the uranium nuclei had been split into new particles. Meitner, along with her nephew Otto Frisch, coined the term "fission" to describe what had occurred with the uranium nucleus. They drew an analogy to a water drop dividing in two. Meitner and Frisch also theorized the potential for a chain reaction and thus, an atomic bomb.

On January 26, 1939, Danish physicist Niels Bohr announced the discoveries of Lise Meitner and her German colleagues to a physics conference at the George Washington University in Washington, DC. After learning about "atomic fission," using uranium, some attendees immediately set up an experiment to replicate the results at the nearby Carnegie Institution of Science. The race for the bomb had begun.

A RACE WITH HITLER'S SCIENTISTS
Glenn Seaborg was motivated by the urgency of World War II.
"Lots of signs made us think that we were in a losing race with Hitler's scientists. We understood full well what it would have meant if Adolf Hitler had got the atomic bomb before the Allies did."
Interview with Academy of Achievement
September 1990

GENERAL GROVES: COOL, CONFIDENT AND DECISIVE

"My emotional graph is a straight line. I never worried. This job would never have been done if I had. I never had any doubts. Not having any doubts, I could not feel very surprised or elated by our success."

"If I can't do the job, no one man can."
Interview in Collier's *magazine*
October 1945

Photo courtesy of the U.S. Department of Energy

The project's pace quickened with the selection of hard-driving U.S. Army Corps of Engineers General Leslie R. Groves to direct the project in September 1942. Groves had been in charge of all domestic Army construction needed to mobilize for the war, including the mammoth Pentagon building.

Groves was supremely self-confident, extraordinarily decisive and insightful. He was also an astute judge of people. Despite J. Robert Oppenheimer's past communist associations and lack of management experience, Groves recognized that Oppenheimer was critical to the success of the project and hired him as its scientific director.

A drawing of the Chicago Pile-1
Image from AHF Archives

Enrico Fermi, Leo Szilard and other top physicists joined the Manhattan Project effort at the Metallurgical Laboratory or "Met Lab" housed at the University of Chicago. Under the bleachers of Stagg Field, a university stadium, the world's first controlled, self-sustaining nuclear chain reaction took place in a squash court on December 2, 1942.

The Manhattan Project began as a small research program. At the outset, J. Robert Oppenheimer estimated that 100 scientists could do the research, design and testing at Los Alamos.

But the endeavor proved to be far more complex, involving not just scientific research but a gargantuan engineering and industrial effort. Mammoth first-of-a-kind factories were built to produce the fissile material at the core of the bombs, enriched uranium and plutonium.

The hulking K-25 plant at Oak Ridge, TN, was one mile long, built to separate the isotopes of uranium using gaseous diffusion. A totally different approach involved huge "Calutrons," named after the University of California's newly invented "cyclotrons." The Calutrons used electromagnetic forces to separate the isotopes. A third technique, thermal separation, required a third huge facility to produce enriched uranium. At Hanford, WA, three huge reactors and chemical separation facilities were constructed to produce plutonium.

Dozens of small manufacturers, major corporations and universities contributed. As Danish physicist Niels Bohr predicted, the entire country became a huge factory.

The K-25 Plant in Oak Ridge, Tennessee
Photo courtesy of the U.S. Department of Energy

EN ROUTE TO LOS ALAMOS

Arriving in New Mexico
LAMY

The Lamy train station looks pretty much the same today as it did in World War II. Ten miles from Santa Fe, Lamy is the nearest stop on the former Atchinson, Topeka and Santa Fe Railway. As reflected in these accounts, young men and women assigned to work at Los Alamos arrived not knowing where they were or where they were going.

WITH A PILLBOX HAT AND PRECIOUS NYLONS

In 1943, Becky Bradford Diven was 25 years old and working in the sub-basement of the California Institute of Technology on a quartz fiber project. After two years, she told her supervisor that she was going to quit. Instead she received this offer: "We have a job, we can't tell you what it is, where it is, but they want you to come and do quartz fiber work." Soon after accepting the job, she was traveling from Pasadena by train to Los Alamos and would be met at Lamy.

"So I dressed with care, a little pillbox with a veil, my precious nylons, high heels, and I was ready to go to Los Alamos. Well, I stood on the platform [at Lamy] and waited and waited. Finally a WAC [member of the Women's Army Corps] came up and said, 'Are you Becky Diven?'

'Yeah.' Later I discovered they said, 'She's never going to last here.'"
~Atomic Heritage Foundation oral history, April 8, 2003

Lamy station today

"JUST STAY ON THE TRAIN"

After being sent to the Army Specialized Training Program in Ohio, and then Oak Ridge, TN, Jay Wechsler was told, "Grab your gear, you're leaving." He ended up on a train car heading West. "We had no idea where we were going...There were no officers in charge of anything and no instructions—just stay on the train...During the wartime, most of the towns had all of their signs removed...So we had no idea where we were, although someone said it was New Mexico.

"I think we had been on that railroad car for three and a half days by that time and it hadn't been serviced in any way...The train stopped... [and] it looked like there was nothing there at that stop.

"There was a 6x6 vehicle and we unloaded and boarded it. We still didn't know where we were. Headed off down the highway and ended up coming into Santa Fe but we didn't know it was Santa Fe. Every time the truck slowed up, we would ask people 'Where are we?' and they would look at us very strangely and nobody answered...We had no idea that that was where we were going or what it was."

EN ROUTE TO "LOST ALAMOS"

John Mench was told he was "pre-assigned to Manhattan District" and ordered to proceed to Lamy, NM. After three days on the train, "I finally arrived in Lamy in the evening. I went into the little station at Lamy. There was only one man at the station. Nothing else within miles. So I said, 'Where is the telephone?' He said, 'Over there in the corner'...I was told [by the officer] to sit in a certain seat at the station—there were only three seats anyway—and the sergeant picked me up in a couple of hours. By this time, it was almost dark...

I woke up the next morning to this place called 'Lost Alamos' which was the G.I. name for Los Alamos. There was nothing I could see but mud, boardwalks, log cabin buildings, beautiful scenery and security fences."

~Excerpts from AHF oral histories, April 2003

109 East Palace
SANTA FE

Scientists, engineers, Women's Army Corps, military police and all others assigned to work on the top-secret project at Los Alamos were directed to 109 E. Palace Avenue in Santa Fe after arriving in New Mexico. The building, constructed as a Spanish hacienda in the 1600s, is located just off the plaza in downtown Santa Fe. During World War II, it was the administrative hub of the Manhattan Project.

109 East Palace Today
Photo courtesy of the Santa Fe New Mexican

Dorothy Scarritt McKibbin was the first reassuring face the fatigued newcomers saw. At 109 E. Palace, McKibbin informed them that their journey continued another 35 miles along the winding road up to the Pajarito Plateau. In the early months, she dispatched an average of 65 people each day to "the Hill," as Los Alamos was called.

The steady stream of arrivals meant the office was often "bedlam," as McKibbin described it. She issued passes and IDs and directed newcomers to their homes, received shipments of household items to be distributed to the Hill's residents, and tended to personal matters as needed.

Born in Kansas City, MO, in 1897, McKibbin graduated from Smith College in 1919 where she had been class president and active in raising funds for World War I refugees. She first visited New Mexico in 1926 when her doctor sent her to New Mexico to recover from tuberculosis. In 1927, she married Joseph McKibbin and had a son, Kevin, in 1930. Tragically, her husband died of Hodgkin's disease in 1931, prompting Dorothy to move to Santa Fe with her son.

She was captivated by the beauty of the area and the genuine hospitality of its people. She worked for the Spanish and Indian Trading Company for ten years where she developed an appreciation for Native American arts and crafts.

In 1942, McKibbin was 45 years old and interested in helping with the war effort. She was immediately taken by Oppenheimer when they met and accepted his job offer. As Oppenheimer's secretary Priscilla Greene recalled, "We were all completely under his spell."

McKibbin was the perfect person for her job and quickly became indispensable as the "Gatekeeper" at 109 E. Palace Avenue and a close friend and confidante of Oppenheimer. She had a warm smile, an engaging personality and was reassuringly calm and efficient. In recognition of her contribution, McKibbin was awarded the title of "First Lady" of Los Alamos and declared a Living Treasure of Santa Fe.

Dorothy often attended parties at the Oppenheimer house. She is pictured here with Oppenheimer and Victor Weisskopf (right).
Photo courtesy of the U.S. Department of Energy

La Fonda
100 EAST SAN FRANCISCO STREET, SANTA FE

An inn has been located at this address across the street from the Plaza and at the terminus of the Santa Fe Trail since the 1800s. The present La Fonda (Spanish for "inn") was built in 1922.

During the Manhattan Project, La Fonda was a favorite watering hole for the scientists and their wives who ventured down from the Hill for a taste of civilization. Fearing that they might loosen up too much and reveal the project's top-secret goal, covert government agents monitored Los Alamos residents as they unwound here. Santa Feans were trying to figure out what the secret project was at Los Alamos. Worried that they might guess correctly, Oppenheimer asked physicists Bob Serber and John Manley to go to Santa Fe with their wives to spread the rumor that Los Alamos was making electric rockets.

La Fonda Hotel
Image courtesy of Wikimedia Commons

LOS ALAMOS: THE FORBIDDEN NAME
"The obvious place to go was the bar of La Fonda Hotel since it is a favorite with local businessmen as well as with the tourist trade. We arrived there about 9 PM feeling a little silly and self-conscious...Our conversation was singular dull as we each wondered how to bring electric rockets into it. We told little stories about Los Alamos, mentioning the forbidden name boldly and loudly. But no ears cocked in our direction; no one peered around us. A few bored people quietly sipped their drinks and showed not the slightest interest.

"We gave up and started home...We were obviously flops at building an electric rocket...We would stick to the atomic bomb."
~Charlotte Serber, "Labor Pains," in Standing By and Making Do, *62-63*

Castillo Street Bridge
AT PASEO DE PERALTA, SANTA FE

Klaus Fuchs fled Germany for England in 1933. He was one of a few exiled German physicists allowed to work on England's "Tube Alloys" or atomic bomb project. By the time he came to Los Alamos as part of the British Mission in 1944, he was already engaged in espionage.

As Laura Fermi recalled, Fuchs was an attractive young man, polite and well spoken. No one suspected that he was leading a double life and giving secret information to the Soviets.

Klaus Fuchs
Photo courtesy of Wikimedia Commons

Fuchs drove a battered blue Buick to Santa Fe to meet his Soviet agent, Harry Gold. They agreed to rendezvous at the Castillo Street Bridge on Saturday, June 2, 1945. Fuchs met with agent Gold many times over the summer of 1945 and gave the Soviet Union valuable data. Together with two other sources, Fuchs enabled the Soviets to expedite their atomic bomb development by at least two years. In 1950, Fuchs was arrested and spent nine years in jail in England. After his release, Fuchs lived in Dresden, East Germany, where he continued to share atomic and hydrogen bomb secrets with the Chinese.

Prime Minister Clement Atlee, President Harry Truman, and Premier Josef Stalin at the July-August 1945 Potsdam Conference. Stalin already knew of the U.S. efforts to develop an atomic bomb, thanks to the intelligence of Fuchs and other Soviet agents.
Photo by the U.S Army Signal Corps. Courtesy of the National Archives.

The Pueblos
STATE OF NEW MEXICO

Julian and Maria Montoya Martinez
Photo courtesy of the Los Alamos Historical Museum Archives

Northern New Mexico was battered economically by drought and the Depression in the years leading up to World War II. The top-secret project on the Pajarito Plateau provided new opportunities for economic growth in the region. The Pueblos welcomed the economic benefits but have been conflicted as they seek to preserve ancestral identities and traditional ways of life in a changing world.

The nearest of the pueblos, San Ildefonso, provided the bulk of day laborers for Los Alamos. Workers were picked up by bus and rode to the Hill to receive their assignments They worked seven days a week, returning home at sunset. Men were generally employed as truck drivers, construction and maintenance workers, carpenters and gardeners. Women were recruited as maids and childcare providers. Their skills were vital to the Los Alamos community.

Many of the Hill's residents developed an appreciation for the customs and traditions of their Pueblo neighbors. The demand for local crafts, such as pottery, often exceeded the supply. Some artists sacrificed their intricate designs and painting style to keep up with orders.

Maria Montoya Martinez (1887-1980) was probably the most famous of the twentieth century Pueblo potters. She and her husband, Julian, worked together to revive and refine an ancient San Ildefonso technique of black-on-black pottery.

Dancers at the San Ildefonso Pueblo in 1946
Courtesy of the Bretscher Papers, Churchill College, Cambridge

The residents of Los Alamos also began to attend Pueblo feast days. During these celebrations, they were often invited to eat in Pueblo homes and watch dances. Ultimately, the encounter between Pueblo nations and the Los Alamos community produced a mixed legacy.

The Pueblo community became increasingly dependent on the outside world. Local economies shifted from a centuries-old subsistence or bartering economy to a cash-based or "plutonium economy."

With their proximity to the laboratory, San Ildefonso, Santa Clara, Jemez and Cochiti leaders have had longstanding concerns over the impact of the laboratory on their lands and community. Since the 1990s, these pueblos have had financial support from the Department of Energy to assess environmental impacts and participate in cleanup decisions.

Then as now, local leaders recognize that the job opportunities of the laboratory, the growing tourist trade and broader cultural assimilation into New Mexico life have had benefits. The struggle to reconcile these benefits with the preservation of ancestral identities and ways of life continues to be an important dimension of the Manhattan Project's legacy in northern New Mexico.

Otowi Bridge
HIGHWAY 502 OVER RIO GRANDE, SANTA FE COUNTY

For more than twenty years, Edith Warner and her companion Atilano Montoya (nicknamed "Tilano"), an elder of the nearby San Ildefonso Pueblo, lived in a small adobe house next to the Otowi Suspension Bridge. "Otowi" in Tewa means "the gap where water sinks." The house became a cultural crossroads between local ways of life and the Manhattan Project.

From 1928 to 1941, Warner was in charge of meeting the "Chili Line" railroad on its way to and from Santa Fe. With the outbreak of World War II, the train service ended. Warner agreed to Oppenheimer's request to serve meals exclusively to Los Alamos scientists and their families in 1943.

Otowi Bridge
Photo courtesy of the Los Alamos Historical Museum Archives

Dinner at the house at Otowi Bridge was booked weeks in advance. The house was decorated with beautiful Native American artifacts, pottery and paintings. Up to ten guests dined together at a single long, carved table. The natural light from the fireplace filled the room with a cozy glow. The food was simple and delicious: a stew with fresh herbs; *posole*, a Native American dish made with parched corn; poached fruit; and Warner's magical chocolate cake.

Warner never asked her guests about the purpose of the labo-

Edith Warner
Photo courtesy of the family of Edith Warner

ratory, although she wrote that she "suspected it was atomic research." After the bombing of Japan in 1945, Warner told her friends: "Much was now explained."

Edith Warner was cherished by the Manhattan Project scientists, including Niels Bohr and Robert Oppenheimer, and their families. She was also beloved by many in the San Ildefonso Pueblo.

New Mexican author Peggy Pond Church memorialized Edith Warner in the charming account *The House at Otowi Bridge*, published in 1959.

EDITH WARNER'S "HUNGRY SCIENTISTS"

"One day in the 1930s a young man [Oppenheimer] came riding by on his horse, from his ranch in the Pecos Valley, and stopped for refreshment. He stayed all afternoon, and thus began a friendship that culminated in our dinners at Miss Warner's during the war, and which also, by an ironic twist of fate, brought the atomic bomb project to her very door. She became much concerned with the new atomic age and the direction it would take in the future…"

"Miss Warner preferred only 10 for dinner, but if a VIP suddenly came up to the site, she would stretch the reservations, particularly for her favorites, 'Uncle Nick' Bohr and his son, Aage. The atmosphere was one of quiet talk. She frowned on any loud voices, and once scolded Jane Wilson and Genia Peierls for talking too loudly about Mesa affairs when Bohr was also a guest…"

"She called us her 'hungry scientists,' a term well earned by the generous amount of her good food we consumed. Everything was home-grown, home-cooked, and tasted delicious."

~*Bernice Brode,* Tales of Los Alamos, *120-123*

ASHLEY POND IN LOS ALAMOS: *Pictured in 1924, 1946, and 2005*
Photos courtesy of the Los Alamos Historical Museum Archives, Bretscher Papers at Churchill College, Cambridge, and Democracy for New Mexico (top to bottom)

LOS ALAMOS

P.O. Box 1663
FORMERLY AT 108 CATHEDRAL PLACE, SANTA FE

Los Alamos was so secret that it was not on any map. No one who went to live and work at Los Alamos was allowed to tell friends or family members where they were going. As Ruth Marshak's husband Robert explained, "I can tell you nothing about it. We're going away, that's all."

A single post office box, P.O. Box 1663, served all Los Alamos's residents. Babies born during the Manhattan Project had "P.O. Box 1663" listed as their birthplace on their birth certificates. Sears & Roebuck delivery men became suspicious when orders for a dozen baby bassinets came from the same address. By the end of the war, five thousand people were assigned P.O. Box 1663.

Aerial view of "P.O. Box 1663," Los Alamos, NM
Photo courtesy of the U.S. Department of Energy

THE TOP-SECRET WAR

"The secrecy was remarkable…We were not allowed to have contact with the outside world. One time a cousin of mine from New York wrote to me…She said, "I am coming to Santa Fe for a short vacation. Can we get together?" I showed the letter to the censors office…and I said, "How do I respond to this?" Everything incoming and outgoing went through the censors' office. And they said, "All you can say is, 'I'm sorry I can't see you. Period.' No reason. My cousin was very miffed until she found out after the war what the reason was."

~Gerhart Friedlander, AHF oral history, April 27, 2002

Fuller Lodge
2132 CENTRAL AVENUE, LOS ALAMOS

Photo courtesy of the Los Alamos Historical Museum Archives

Fuller Lodge was constructed as part of the Los Alamos Ranch School in 1928. John Gaw Meem, one of the leading architects of the Southwest, designed it using vertical ponderosa pine logs and native stone. The school used it as a dining room and recreational hall.

After the U.S. Government took over the property, the lodge was used as a dining hall and guest quarters for Manhattan Project personnel. It was also the center of social activity for the scientists and their families. On Saturday nights, the lodge was often packed with people enjoying square dancing, concerts or plays. It continues to be an important social center for the Los Alamos community.

SERVING STANDARDS
"Besides the PXs [Post Exchanges], one could eat at Fuller Lodge, which would serve splendid food for months and then slump back to its usual standard of mediocre cooking."
~Ruth Marshak, "Secret City," Standing By and Making Do, *12*

Bathtub Row
LOS ALAMOS

Just beyond Fuller Lodge, Bathtub Row was prized real estate. Six cottages built by the Los Alamos Ranch School for the masters were originally expected to house the majority of the scientific staff. Early estimates of how many staff would be needed were off by thousands. These cottages fit at most a dozen of the top-echelon laboratory and military officials.

To the envy of the rest of Los Alamos, the homes were equipped with bathtubs, earning them the nickname "bathtub row." The Baker House is where Sir James Chadwick, head of the British Mission, lived (T-128). Unfortunately, Mrs. Chadwick preferred Washington, DC, and he spent more time there conferring with General Groves.

The Baker House, where Sir James Chadwick lived (T-128)

ADDITIONAL INFORMATION
To learn more, stop by the Los Alamos Historical Society Museum, located in one of the original guest houses next to Fuller Lodge, or visit online at http://www.losalamoshistory.org.

The Arts and Crafts Cottage, where Ashbridge, Fermi, and Bradbury resided (T-114)
Photo courtesy of the Los Alamos Historical Museum Archives

Director of the Trinity site Kenneth Bainbridge lived in Spruce Cottage (T-115). The Arts and Crafts Cottage (T-114) housed during or after the war Lieutenant Colonel Whitney Ashbridge, the military commander who oversaw both military and civilian life in Los Alamos; Italian physicist Enrico Fermi; and laboratory director Norris Bradbury.

Other Bathtub Row cottages housed physicists Edwin McMillan and Hans Bethe (T-112), the Robert Oppenheimer family (T-111), and Capt. William Parsons across the street (T-110).

Master Cottage #1, where the Bethes lived during the war (T-112)
Photo courtesy of the Los Alamos Historical Museum Archives

Oppenheimer House
BATHTUB ROW & PEACH STREET, LOS ALAMOS

Oppenheimer and his wife Kitty lived in this modest Bathtub Row cottage with their son Peter, born May 12, 1941, and baby daughter Katherine ("Tyke," later "Toni"), born December 7, 1944, at Los Alamos. The two children probably slept in the glassed-in sleeping porch while the parents slept in the bedroom that doubled as a study.

The Oppenheimer house was built in 1929 for artist May Connell, sister of the Ranch School director, and the living room (left and below) was her studio. The Oppenheimers occasionally used the room to entertain. Many scientists played

musical instruments, including physicist Edward Teller, who enjoyed playing the piano. If the Oppenheimer parties grew too large, people spilled out on the lawn. Oppenheimer often asked the military police to declare the entire area "secure" so the guests could freely discuss their top-secret work on the bomb.

> **OPPENHEIMER AT PLAY**
> Oppenheimer's 39th birthday party was the first large celebration of residents on the Hill. The project's director was known for supplying plenty to drink and less to eat. According to Louis Hempelmann, "The alcohol hits you harder at 8,000 feet, so everybody, even the most sober people, like [physicist I.I.] Rabi, was [*sic*] just feeling no pain at all. Everyone was dancing."
> ~*Kai Bird and Martin Sherwin,* American Prometheus, *256-257*

The front door of Oppenheimer's house

> **OPPENHEIMER THE COOK**
> "At home, Oppie was the cook. He was still partial to exotic hot dishes like *nasi goreng*, but one of his stock dinners included steak, fresh asparagus and potatoes, prefaced by a gin sour or martini."
> ~*Kai Bird and Martin Sherwin,* American Prometheus, *256*

Los Alamos the Boomtown
BATHTUB ROW & BEYOND

CONSTRUCTION BOOM

"Hundreds of scientists and their families had to settle for lesser accommodations. The pace of housing construction was frenetic. In 1943, the first wave of Manhattan Project scientists were housed in drab duplex and quadruplex apartments called Sundts. In 1944, the next wave were assigned to smaller Morganville homes built on the treeless mesa east of Bathtub Row. These were followed by single-family homes in an area dubbed McKeeville. While none of these options received rave reviews, the Special Engineer Detachment, Women's Army Corps, military police, and support staff were often relegated to huts, trailers, dorms and barracks."

~*Craig Martin,* Quads, Shoeboxes and Sunken Living Rooms

Barracks on West Road, Summer 1946
Photo courtesy of the Bretscher Papers, Churchill College, Cambridge

BABY BOOM

The majority of Los Alamos residents were in their twenties and thirties; those who were in their forties considered themselves the community's elders. One unanticipated consequence of these demographics was a baby boom, much to General Groves' consternation. The Los Alamos residents joked with the following limerick:

"The General's in a stew, he trusted you and you;
He thought you'd be scientific, instead you're just prolific
And what is he to do?"

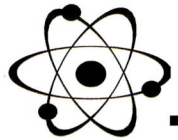

Perro Caliente
THE PECOS WILDERNESS

The Perro Caliente cabin loved by the Oppenheimers
Photo courtesy of the Los Alamos Historical Museum Archives

In July 1928, J. Robert Oppenheimer, his brother Frank, and their friend Katherine Page went for a horsback ride up into the Pecos mountains above Los Pinos. At 9,500 feet, they stumbled upon a rustic cabin. Oppenheimer immediately fell in love with the small cabin made of half-trunks and adobe mortar.

When Page told Oppenheimer that the cabin, along with 154 acres of land, were for rent, he happily exclaimed, "Hot dog!" The Oppenheimers playfully dubbed the picturesque cabin "Perro Caliente," Spanish for "hot dog," upon leasing it. In 1947, Oppenheimer purchased Perro Caliente for $10,000.

Oppenheimer used the cabin as a place to sleep in between long, scenic horseback rides. Many physicists, from the Serbers to Ernest Lawrence to Victor Weisskopf, spent time at the cabin. Oppenheimer reveled in the tranquility provided by the remote and spartan cabin, nestled in the spectacular Pecos mountains.

In the summer of 1940, Oppenheimer invited his paramour, Kitty Harrison, to Perro Caliente. Their son, Peter--whom Robert mischievously nicknamed "Pronto"--was born in May 1941 and was likely conceived in the cabin. The cabin is still owned by the Oppenheimer family.

The V-Site
TA-16-516 and TA-16-517, LOS ALAMOS

Located in a bucolic setting surrounded by tall pines, these humble wooden and asbestos-shingled buildings were where the world's first atomic device was assembled. Here scientists, engineers, explosives experts and their young apprentices worked around the clock on the "Gadget," the first plutonium-based atomic explosive.

The restored V-Site
Photo courtesy of the Los Alamos National Laboratory

Glenn Seaborg and his team at Berkeley discovered plutonium in 1940. The first quantities produced by the reactor in Oak Ridge, TN, arrived in Los Alamos in early 1944. But the product was too fissile to use in the weapon designed for uranium. Instead, scientists had to accelerate work on an alternative.

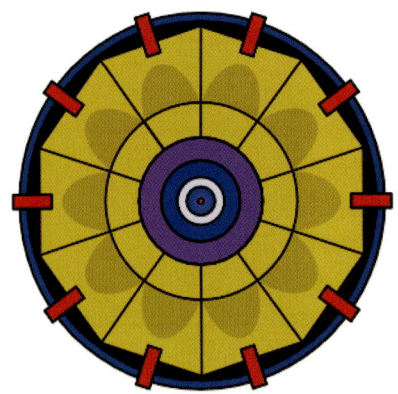

The original V-Site buildings were fortified by mounds of earth to protect them against accidental explosions. High explosives were melted, mixed and poured into molds at neighboring S-Site to produce the lenses that surrounded a core of plutonium.

The lenses create a shock wave that compresses the plutonium. At the very center, an "initiator" releases a burst of neutrons.
Image courtesy of Wikimedia Commons

The Gadget onstage at the opera *Doctor Atomic* and the actual device in a 1945 photo
Photos courtesy of the Metropolitan Opera and Martin Miller

The 32 lenses were fitted together like a soccer ball. Each lens had to be detonated at precisely the same time. A shock wave compressed the core to bring the plutonium to a critical mass. The energy released was equivalent to 21 kilotons of TNT. This painstaking assembly was accomplished at the V-Site behind a "no peek" fence. Once completed, the Gadget was tested on July 16, 1945, at the Trinity site near Alamogordo, NM.

President Harry Truman was meeting at Potsdam, Germany, when he received word of the successful test. Truman confided the news of the enormously powerful new weapon to Soviet leader Joseph Stalin and was surprised by his lack of response. Stalin, it turns out, already knew all about the American bomb program through espionage.

The V-Site was awarded a Save America's Treasures grant by the National Park Service in 1999 after being slated for demolition. However, the Cerro Grande Fire in May 2000 destroyed all but two of the original buildings.

The V-Site was restored in 2006 after the Atomic Heritage Foundation raised the matching funds for the grant. In 2008, the National Trust for Historic Preservation honored the V-Site Restoration Project with a National Trust/Advisory Council on Historic Preservation Award for Federal Partnerships in Historic Preservation.

The Gun Site
TA-8-1, LOS ALAMOS

The Gun Site (TA-8-1) was where Manhattan Project scientists and engineers developed and tested the gun-type weapon design. The design for the "Little Boy" bomb dropped on Hiroshima on August 6, 1945, was developed here. In 2001, the Department of Energy named the Gun Site one of its "Signature Facilities of the Manhattan Project." Plans are in place to restore the site.

The Gun Site includes three concrete "bombproof" buildings built in a ravine. This 3,200 square foot bunker-like building was the main work area.

The gun design was straightforward. Basically, a "bullet" of nuclear material was fired at very high speed into a second nuclear mass, creating a critical mass. This released enormous energy with an immense explosion. Scientists were confident the design would work and the gun-type bomb was not tested before it was used against Japan.

The work on the gun-type bomb illustrates the complexity and uncertainty of the project. At the outset, scientists assumed that this design would work with either uranium or plutonium. In the spring of 1944, the Los Alamos team discovered that the plutonium (Pu-239) produced by the reactor in Oak Ridge, TN, contained an impurity (Pu-240), that would spontaneously fission. Scientists predicted the plutonium would predetonate before the "bullet" reached its target and the bomb would fizzle instead of exploding.

In the summer of 1944, director Robert Oppenheimer ordered a major reorganization of the laboratory to focus on an alternative weapon design for plutonium. It was a desperate and necessary decision. In early August 1945, the Manhattan Project had only enough of each type of fissionable material for one Little Boy (uranium) and one Fat Man (plutonium). Material for another plutonium bomb was about ten days behind.

The Gun Site had a large proving ground above the bunker-like buildings. Two Naval cannons were hidden from view by wooden housing on rails. The housing could be removed when the cannons were fired. The team observed the firings from the bunkers through a periscope mounted in a 45-foot tower. After a test firing, they retrieved the projectiles and analyzed the test results in a work area equipped with a camera room, darkroom and X-ray equipment. Work is underway to restore the facilities as they were during the Manhattan Project.

An artist's rendition of what the restored Gun Site might look like
Image courtesy of the Los Alamos National Laboratory

SOLDIER/SCIENTIST ENLISTED TO WIN

Philip Morrison (1915-2005) was a physicist who arrived at Los Alamos in the summer of 1944. He remembers feeling the "intensity of concern, intensity of work, intensity of hope, intensity of wonder…Most people who came in that '44 crisis felt like soldiers. We were being enlisted to win this battle…everything else would have to go."
~*Interview with Philip Morrison, November 30, 1999*

The Concrete Bowl
TA-6-37, LOS ALAMOS

This 200-foot diameter bowl is testimony to the scientists' doubts as late as 1945 that the plutonium-based implosion bomb design would work. The bomb was much more complex than the gun-type bomb and without computers and modern electronics, the challenges to successful construction were enormous.

Constructed in 1944, the bowl was a means of recovering the precious plutonium if a test failed. Scientists used depleted uranium to test whether the recovery technique worked.

After receiving an early model IBM prototype computer in the spring of 1945, scientists were able to calculate the precise configuration of the explosive lenses for the implosion bomb. In the desert near Alamogordo, NM, on July 16, 1945, the test weapon was detonated with a force equivalent to exploding more than 20 thousand tons of TNT.

A NEARLY IMPOSSIBLE TASK
In 1944, George Kistiakowsky, head of the explosives department, drew a large circle on a blackboard. "This is why you are here. We're going to build an atom bomb and it's going to be an implosion device. We have to make the high explosive lens system that is going to compress this plutonium ball in the center and make it into a supercritical mass...The lenses have to be made very, very precisely and there is still some doubt as to whether it will work."

~Robert Wilson to Tom Zannes in 2001

The concrete bowl, which is 200 feet in diameter
Photo courtesy of the U.S. Department of Energy

Quonset Hut
TA-22-1, LOS ALAMOS

Working under intense time constraints, an effective plutonium-based weapon had been designed, built and tested at Trinity. Before the "Fat Man" bomb was shipped to Tinian Island in the Pacific, some assembly of the bomb's explosive components was done in the Quonset hut.

NAVIGATING BY PITCHES AND TUNES

The 509th Composite Group was responsible for the flights that dropped the atomic bombs. The men practiced with "pumpkin bombs" filled with conventional explosives that were approximately the shape and size of the atomic bomb dropped on Nagasaki.

"We found out that the [509th unit] navigators were practicing a lot [while training in the Southwest] by tuning in on the nearest radio station and listening to the baseball game or some songs, homing on the radio station. Anybody can do that, for heaven's sake! So we sent them all down to Batista Field, Cuba and sent them out on missions over the South Atlantic. One guy said to me, 'Ted, aren't you afraid you're going to lose some of these crews over there?' And I said, 'Would you rather lose them now or when they are on their mission?'"

~Theodore "Dutch" Van Kirk, Navigator on the Enola Gay in Kelly, The Manhattan Project, *326*

The Enola Gay on Tinian
Photo courtesy of the U.S. Department of Energy

Louis Slotin Building
TA-18-1, LOS ALAMOS

The building in which the accident occurred
Photo courtesy of the Los Alamos National Laboratory

At 3:20 PM on Tuesday, May 21, 1946, at the Pajarito Laboratory site, a postwar criticality experiment went terribly wrong. Louis Slotin, a Canadian Manhattan Project scientist, was doomed.

Slotin was "tickling the dragon's tail," performing a criticality experiment that involved gradually bringing together two beryllium-coated halves of a sphere that held plutonium at its core—without allowing the halves to touch—and recording the increasing rate of fissioning. Seven other individuals were in the room when the screwdriver Slotin used to separate the halves slipped.

A blue glow flashed in the room. The Geiger counter clicked furiously. Slotin responded quickly and stopped the chain reaction by knocking the spheres apart. He had been exposed to nearly 1,000 rads of radiation, far more than anyone else in the room and well above a lethal dose. Slotin's health rapidly deteriorated following the accident. He spent the last nine days of his life in the Los Alamos hospital receiving around-the-clock care. Despite heroic attempts to save his life, Slotin passed away on May 30, 1946.

Louis Slotin
Photo courtesy of Center of Science Stories

After Slotin's accident, criticality experiments at Los Alamos were conducted remotely, separating scientists from the radioactive material. The building where the accident happened is a memorial to Slotin and his legacy, a new era of safety procedures.

Pond Cabin
TA-18-29, LOS ALAMOS

The Pond Cabin was built in 1913 by Ashley Pond, a Detroit businessman, as part of a dude ranch (the Pajarito Club) that failed in 1916. The cabin was used as an office for the dude ranch's financial manager.

In 1917, Pond started the Los Alamos Ranch School, which succeeded in educating some 600 boys before the government took over the school in 1943. Italian physicist Emilio Segrè soon joined the Manhattan Project at Los Alamos as a group leader.

Emilio Segrè
Photo courtesy of atomicarchive.com

Segrè decided to use the Pond Cabin and other former Pajarito Club buildings to research spontaneous fission of plutonium and uranium, taking advantage of the canyon's remote location.

The Pond Cabin at TA-18
Photo courtesy of LANS

Segrè's discoveries here regarding U-235 and cosmic rays led to the design of the Little Boy bomb.

Segrè was a student, collaborator and lifelong friend of Enrico Fermi, a Nobel Prize-winning physicist (1938). After the war Fermi and Herbert Anderson founded the Institute for Nuclear Studies at the University of Chicago. Segrè later published a biography of Fermi.

Herbert Anderson and Enrico Fermi outside Segrè's laboratory in the fall of 1945
Photo courtesy of the Bretscher Papers, Churchill College, Cambridge

The Gadget being hoisted at Trinity Site
Photo courtesy of the U.S. Department of Energy

THE TRINITY SITE

McDonald Ranch House
WHITE SANDS MISSILE RANGE

On July 16, 1945, at 5:29:45 AM, scientists tested an atomic bomb for the first time. The site of this history-changing event had humble beginnings.

The McDonald Ranch House

SEARCHING FOR A TEST SITE
Because implosion was much more complicated than gun assembly, the only way to determine if the system would work was to test it. Kenneth T. Bainbridge, a Harvard physicist, was put in charge of preparations for the test. He began searching in April 1944 for a site that would meet General Groves' specifications: remote, approximately 17 by 24 miles and no further from Los Alamos than necessary.

In May 1944, Bainbridge led Oppenheimer on an exploration of unmapped ranch sites in New Mexico, camping along the way. In September, he settled on a site in the Jornada del Muerto, the Journey of Death, part of the Alamogordo Bombing Range. The ranch property was owned by David McDonald. Bainbridge staked out an 18-by-24 mile claim and renovated the ranch house for a field laboratory.

Men sent to prepare for the test had difficulty adjusting to the intense sun and heat. Their only relief was jumping in the cistern. It was a tense time with hundreds of things that could go wrong and jeopardize the project. One of the final tests failed because of breaks in the half-mile long cable buried between the tower and control bunker.

Photo courtesy of Wikimedia Commons

BABYSITTING THE BOMB

Donald F. Hornig recalls the night he spent stationed atop the tower with the Gadget, waiting for a storm to pass over the site.

"Oppenheimer was terribly worried about the fact that the thing was so complicated and so many people knew exactly how it was put together that it would be easy to sabotage. So he thought someone had better baby sit it right up until the moment it was fired. They asked for volunteers and as the youngest guy present, I was selected. I don't know if it was that I was most expendable or best able to climb a 100-foot tower!

"By then there was a violent thunder and lightning storm. I climbed up there, took along a book, *Desert Island Decameron*, and climbed the tower on top of which there was the bomb, all wired up and ready to go. Little metal shack, open on one side, no windows on the other three, and a 60-watt bulb and just a folding chair for me to sit on beside the bomb, and there I was!

"All I had was a telephone. I wasn't equipped to defend myself, I don't know what I was supposed to do. There were no instructions! The possibility of lightning striking the tower was very much on my mind. But it was very wet and the odds were the tower would act like a giant lightning rod and the electricity would just go straight down to the wet desert. In that case, nothing would have happened. The other case was that it would set the bomb off. And in that case, I'd never know about it! So I read my book."

~*Kelly*, The Manhattan Project, *298*
Photos courtesy of the Los Alamos National Laboratory

Ground Zero
WHITE SANDS MISSILE RANGE

Soldiers began arriving at the Trinity test site in December 1944. Risks of the top-secret project being discovered were matched by the scientists' fears of uncontrollable nuclear fallout or worse. Without providing details, General Groves prepared the Governor of New Mexico for a possible evacuation of the state's population.

Artist John Hull painted SEDers watching the blast at Trinity

Ground Zero was located 3,400 yards northwest of the McDonald Ranch House. The plutonium core was assembled in the master bedroom of the house and mated with the implosion assembly at the tower.

Because of violent thunderstorms, the leaders decided to postpone the original detonation time of 0400 hours. The storm raised fears of setting off an accidental explosion. Once the rain and lightning passed, physicist Samuel K. Allison began the countdown. In all, 260 members of the scientific and military community witnessed this historic moment.

The bomb detonated at 5:29:45 AM.

"COMPLETELY BREATHTAKING"
Val Fitch, then a member of the Special Engineer Detachment, recalled:
"It took about 30 millionths of a second for the flash of light...to reach us outside the bunker at south 10,000, the main control. It took the blast wave about 30 seconds. There was the initial loud report, the sharp gust of wind, and then the long period of reverberations as the sound waves echoed off the nearby mountains."
~Val Fitch, AHF oral history, March 26, 2008

Physicist Robert Serber observed: "The grandeur and magnitude of the phenomenon was completely breathtaking."
~Kelly, The Manhattan Project, 310

Photo by Jack Aeby. Courtesy of the U. S. Department of Energy

"THIS IS IT!"
Brigadier General Thomas F. Farrell, deputy to General Leslie R. Groves and responsible for the Trinty test, shared this memory.
"In that brief instant in the remote New Mexico desert the tremendous effort of the brains and brawn of all these people came suddenly and startlingly to the fullest fruition. Dr. Oppenheimer, on whom had rested a very heavy burden, grew tenser as the last seconds ticked off. He scarcely breathed. He held on to a post to steady himself.

"For the last few seconds, he stared directly ahead and then when the announcer shouted "Now!" and there came a tremendous burst of light followed shortly thereafter by the deep growling roar of the explosion, his face relaxed into an expression of tremendous relief...

"The tension in the room let up and all started congratulating each other. Everyone sensed 'This is it!' No matter what might happen now all knew that the impossible scientific job had been done."
~Kelly, The Manhattan Project, 295

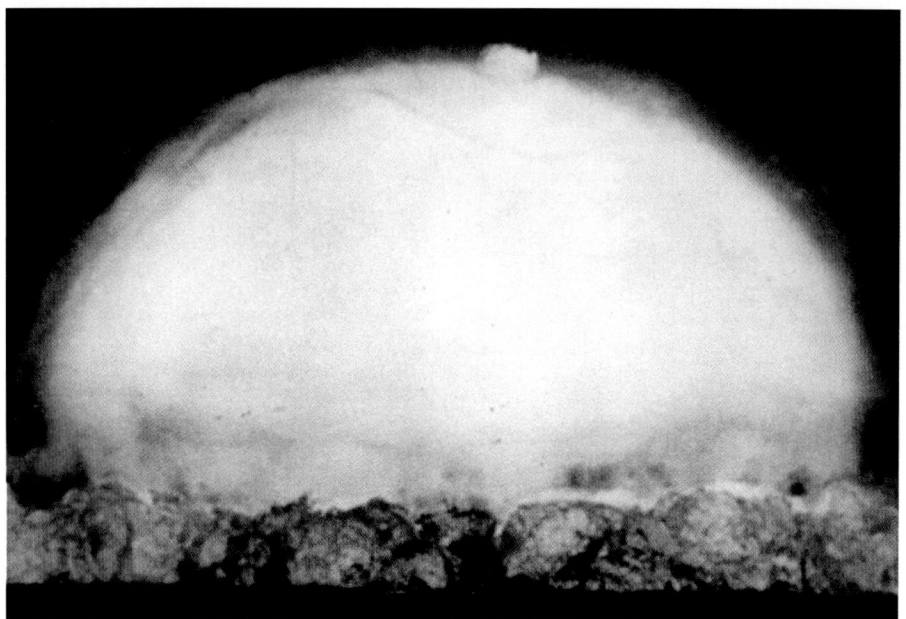

**The Trinity fireball (top) at about 80 milliseconds
and mushroom cloud (bottom) at 15 seconds**
Photos courtesy of the U.S. Department of Energy

Trinity Site
WHITE SANDS MISSILE RANGE

The mushroom cloud rose almost eight miles high and left a crater that was ten feet deep and over 1,000 feet wide. Pieces of a green, glass-like and mildly radioactive mineral were scattered in and around the crater. Dubbed "Trinitite," investigators theorized that desert sand was lifted by the blast, liquefied by the tremendous temperature and rained down on the earth.

Trinitite

Groves (in the center) and Oppenheimer with his signature porkpie hat returned to the Trinity site about six weeks after the explosion on Sunday, September 9, 1945. The twisted metal rods were all that remained of the 100-foot tower. The press was invited for the first time in part to dispel fears of lingering high radiation levels.

In 1952, the site of the first atomic explosion was bulldozed and most of the trinitite removed. The site received a National Historic Landmark designation in 1965 and was listed on the Register of Historic Places less than a year later.

September 1945 press visit to Trinity site
Photo courtesy of the Los Alamos National Laboratory

Jumbo at the Trinity site, 1945. You can see its remains at Trinity today.
Courtesy of the Bretscher Papers, Churchill College, Cambridge

Ground Zero at Trinity is marked by a 12-foot obelisk made of lava rock. Its inscription reads: "Trinity Site: Where the World's First Nuclear Device Was Exploded on July 16, 1945."

You can also see the remains of an 80-ton steel vessel, Jumbo, which was built to contain the precious 13 pounds of plutonium in the event that the bomb failed to detonate. Jumbo illustrates Groves' cautious approach to the project, always having a backup plan.

Because Jumbo was never needed, Groves was concerned that Congress would criticize him for spending $12 million on a white elephant. He ordered that the vessel be destroyed. However, eight 500-pound bombs succeeded only in blowing off its ends.

Monument at Trinity Site
Photo courtesy of LANL

The Trinity Site is open to the public on the first Saturdays in October and April. Eventually, the site may be affiliated with the proposed Manhattan Project National Historical Park and open more often.

Hilton Hotel
125 SECOND STREET NW, ALBUQUERQUE

Previously **La Posada de Albuquerque** and now **Andaluz,** the Hilton Hotel was the site of two important Manhattan Project events. Spy Harry Gold spent the night here before collecting secrets from David Greenglass at Greenglass' apartment. The hotel also served as one of the vantage points from which Manhattan Project officials nervously watched for signs of the top-secret Trinity test on July 16, 1945.

THE SIMPLEST THINGS ARE THE CLEVEREST
David Greenglass, a 22-year-old Army sergeant, was working as a machinist at Los Alamos. He shared his older sister Ethel Rosenberg's communist sympathies and wanted to help the Soviets by providing information on the atomic bomb.

David Greenglass and his wife Ruth
Photo courtesy of the U.S. Department of Energy

Julius Rosenberg devised a signal for David Greenglass and agent Harry Gold. When Gold arrived at Greenglass' 209 High Street apartment, he presented him with half of a raspberry Jell-O boxtop. Greenglass had the other half in his wallet. Snipping the cardboard box in half earlier that year, Julius quipped, "The simplest things are the cleverest."

Gold paid Greenglass $500 and walked away with a package of atomic secrets. Earlier Gold had picked up a package from Klaus Fuchs in Santa Fe that fully described the plutonium bomb. Soviet physicist Igor Kurchatov found the information of great value and was able to accelerate the Soviets' atomic weapons program.

BRIGHTER THAN 150 FLASHBULBS

Thomas O. Jones worked on the Manhattan Project in the Army Counterintelligence Corps at Los Alamos. Jones watched the Trinity explosion from the hotel, 100 miles from the test site.

"My role in the situation was to see whether this bomb went 'pfump' or whether it took half of the state of New Mexico into the air and perhaps into flight around the world. The technical work was proceeding well and it seemed that it would be done on time. That was not my job. My role in that situation was to see that whatever happened, nobody noticed.

Thomas O. Jones
Photo courtesy of AHF Archives

"I spent [the night of the test] with five or six people in a makeshift office in the Hilton Hotel in Albuquerque in a room which faced south where we could see the sky beyond the test site itself over 100 miles away.

Manhattan Project insignia
Image courtesy of AHF Archives

"The [Hilton] room was as if somebody had put off 150 flashbulbs in one hotel room all at once! And as that faded, one realized that the entire sky out there was filling with a bright red which lingered long and faded very gradually."

General Groves sent a coded message to his secretary: "Operated on this morning. Diagnosis not yet complete but results seem satisfactory and already exceed expectations. Local press release necessary as interest extends a great distance. Dr. Groves pleased."
~*Norris,* Racing for the Bomb, *406*

**J. Robert Oppenheimer and General Leslie R. Groves
immortalized by Susanne Vertel in bronze in Los Alamos**
Photo courtesy of the Los Alamos Historical Museum Archives

Sources
AND FURTHER READING

Behind Tall Fences: Stories and Experiences About Los Alamos at its Beginning. Los Alamos: Los Alamos Historical Society, 1996.

Bird, Kai and Martin J. Sherwin. *American Prometheus: The Triumph and Tragedy of J. Robert Oppenheimer.* New York: Vintage Books, 2005.

Brode, Bernice. *Tales of Los Alamos: Life on the Mesa, 1943-1945.* Los Alamos: Los Alamos Historical Society, 1997.

Church, Peggy Pond. *The House at Otowi Bridge: The Story of Edith Warner and Los Alamos.* Albuquerque: The University of New Mexico Press, 1960.

Conant, Jennet. *109 East Palace: Robert Oppenheimer and the Secret City of Los Alamos.* New York: Simon & Schuster, 2005.

Coster-Mullen, John. *Atom Bombs: The Top Secret Inside Story of Little Boy and Fat Man.* Privately published, 2010.

Hevly, Bruce and John M. Findlay. *The Atomic West.* Seattle: University of Washington Press, 1998.

Hunner, Jon. *Inventing Los Alamos: The Growth of an Atomic Community.* Norman: University of Oklahoma Press, 2004.

Johnson, George. *Fire in the Mind: Science, Faith, and the Search for Order.* New York: Random House, 1995.

Kelly, Cynthia C., ed. *The Manhattan Project: The Birth of the Atomic Bomb in the Words of Its Creators, Eyewitnesses and Historians.* New York: Black Dog & Leventhal, 2007.

Lanouette, William. *Genius in the Shadows: A Biography of Leo Szilard, The Man Behind the Bomb.* Chicago: The University of Chicago Press, 1994.

Martin, Craig. *Quads, Shoeboxes and Sunken Living Rooms*. Los Alamos: Los Alamos Historical Society, 2000.

Mason, Katrina R. *Children of Los Alamos: An Oral History of the Town Where the Atomic Age Began*. New York: Twayne Publishers, 1995.

Merlan, Thomas. *Life at Trinity Base Camp*. 2001. Prepared for White Sands Missile Range, New Mexico. Contract No. DAAD07-97-D 0104. Delivery Order No. 30. HS Report No. 9831. White Sands Missile Range Archaeological Research Report No. 01-07.

Norris, Robert S. *Racing for the Bomb: General Leslie R. Groves, the Manhattan Project's Indispensable Man*. South Royalton: Steerforth Press, 2002.

Rhodes, Richard. *The Making of the Atomic Bomb*. New York: Simon & Schuster, 1986.

Rogers, Everett M. and Nancy R. Bartlit. *Silent Voices of World War II: When Sons of the Land of Enchantment Met Sons of the Land of the Rising Sun*. Santa Fe: Sunstone Press, 2005.

Rothman, Hal K. *On Rims & Ridges: The Los Alamos Area since 1880*. Lincoln: University of Nebraska Press, 1992.

Serber, Robert. *The Los Alamos Primer: The First Lectures on How to Build an Atomic Bomb*. Berkeley: University of California Press, 1992.

Steeper, Nancy Cook. *Dorothy Scarritt McKibbin: Gatekeeper to Los Alamos*. Los Alamos Historical Society: Los Alamos, 2003.

Szasz, Ferenc. *The Day the Sun Rose Twice*. Albuquerque: University of New Mexico Press, 1984.

Walker, Stephen. *Shockwave*. New York: HarperCollins, 2005.

Wilson, Jane S. and Charlotte Serber, eds. *Standing By and Making Do: Women of Wartime Los Alamos*. Los Alamos: Los Alamos Historical Society, 1997.

Chronology
THE MAKING OF THE ATOMIC BOMB

1899	New Zealand physicist Ernest Rutherford identifies two kinds of natural radiation: alpha particles and beta rays.
1905	Albert Einstein proposes a theory, shown most dramatically in a nuclear explosion, that defines the relationship between energy and mass: $E=mc^2$.
1932	British physicist James Chadwick discovers the neutron.
1933	Hungarian physicist Leo Szilard first conceives of a nuclear chain reaction and the potential for an atomic bomb.
1934	Italian physicist Enrico Fermi and his team in Rome bombard elements with neutrons and split uranium but do not realize it.
1938	Otto Hahn and Fritz Strassmann, German physicists, discover the fission process by splitting uranium in two. Austrian physicists Lise Meitner and Otto Frisch coin the term "nuclear fission" and publish results.
1939	Danish physicist Niels Bohr announces recent discoveries about fission by European colleagues at an international conference on theoretical physics in Washington, DC.
Aug. 2, 1939	Einstein sends a letter to President Franklin D. Roosevelt warning of the prospect of Germany developing an atomic bomb.
Sept. 1, 1939	Nazi Germany invades Poland; World War II begins.
June 1940	The National Defense Research Committee (NDRC) is established to organize U.S. scientific resources for war, including research on the atom and the fission of uranium.
Feb. 24, 1941	American scientist Glenn T. Seaborg's research team discovers plutonium.
June 22, 1941	Nazi Germany invades the Soviet Union.

Oct. 9, 1941	President Roosevelt asks the Chairman of the NDRC, Vannevar Bush, to determine the cost of an atomic bomb and explore construction needs with the Army.
Dec. 7, 1941	Japan attacks Pearl Harbor.
Dec. 8, 1941	The United States Congress declares war on Japan.
Dec. 10, 1941	Germany and Italy declare war on the United States.
Jan. 19, 1942	President Roosevelt approves the production of an atomic bomb.
Aug. 13, 1942	General order is issued by the Chief of Engineers formally establishing the Manhattan Engineer District (MED) for construction of an atomic bomb.
Sept. 17, 1942	Colonel Leslie R. Groves takes over command of the MED.
Sept. 19, 1942	Groves selects Oak Ridge, TN, as the site for a pilot plant for uranium isotope separation.
Nov. 25, 1942	Groves selects Los Alamos, NM, as the site for a scientific research laboratory, codenamed "Project Y." J. Robert Oppenheimer is chosen as laboratory director.
Dec. 2, 1942	Fermi's team produces the first sustained nuclear fission chain reaction under the bleachers at University of Chicago's Stagg Field.
Jan. 16, 1943	Groves selects Hanford, WA, as a site for plutonium production.
July 17, 1944	Major reorganization to maximize plutonium implosion research occurs at Los Alamos after the plutonium gun-type bomb is abandoned.
April 12, 1945	Franklin D. Roosevelt dies and Harry S. Truman becomes President.
April 25, 1945	Groves and Secretary of War Henry Stimson brief Truman on the Manhattan Project.
May 7, 1945	Nazi Germany surrenders to the Allies.

June 6, 1945	Stimson and other members of the Interim Committee recommend to President Truman that the atomic bomb be used as soon as possible without warning.
June 1945	The Franck Report, urging demonstration of the bomb before military use, begins circulating among scientists.
July 16, 1945	Trinity test, the first nuclear explosion, is successfully conducted in Alamogordo, NM.
July 17, 1945	Potsdam Conference of President Truman, Prime Minister Winston Churchill and Communist Party General Secretary Joseph Stalin begins.
July 21, 1945	Truman approves order for the use of atomic bombs.
July 24, 1945	Truman informs Stalin that the United States has developed a powerful new weapon.
July 26, 1945	Potsdam Declaration asks Japan for unconditional surrender and warns of "prompt and utter destruction."
July 29, 1945	Japan rejects the Potsdam Declaration.
Aug. 6, 1945	The Little Boy uranium bomb is dropped on Hiroshima, Japan.
Aug. 9, 1945	The Fat Man plutonium bomb is dropped on Nagasaki, Japan.
Aug. 14, 1945	Japan surrenders.
Jan. 24, 1946	The United Nations adopts its first resolution, which establishes the United Nations Atomic Energy Commission.
May 21, 1946	Louis Slotin receives a lethal dose of radiation conducting an experiment at Los Alamos. He dies on May 30, 1946.
Aug. 1, 1946	President Truman establishes the Atomic Energy Commission (AEC), which assumes responsibility for all property in the custody and control of the MED.
Aug. 15, 1947	The Manhattan Engineer District is abolished.

Places to See

LOS ALAMOS

BRADBURY SCIENCE MUSEUM
1350 Central Avenue
(505) 667-4444
www.lanl.gov/museum

LOS ALAMOS HISTORICAL MUSEUM
1050 Bathtub Row
(505) 662-6272
www.losalamoshistory.org

BANDELIER NATIONAL MONUMENT
15 Entrance Road
(505) 672-3861 x517
www.nps.gov/band/

SANTA FE

NEW MEXICO HISTORY MUSEUM
113 Lincoln Avenue
(505) 476-5200
www.nmhistorymuseum.org

NEW MEXICO TOURISM DEPARTMENT
491 Old Santa Fe Trail
(505) 827-7400
www.newmexico.org

ALBUQUERQUE

NATIONAL MUSEUM OF NUCLEAR SCIENCE & HISTORY
601 Eubank Boulevard SE
(505) 245-2137
www.nuclearmuseum.org

INDIAN PUEBLO CULTURAL CENTER
2401 12th Street NW
1-866-855-7902
www.indianpueblo.org

OTHER SITES & TOURS

TRINITY SITE
White Sands Missile Range, NM
(575) 678-1134
http://www.wsmr.army.mil/PAO/Trinity/Pages/default.aspx

HISTORIC WENDOVER AIRFIELD MUSEUM
345 South Airport Apron, Wendover, UT
www.wendoverairbase.com

BUFFALO TOURS
Tour the Atomic City of Los Alamos and Surrounding Areas
(505) 662-3965
http://home.covad.net/buffalo-tours/tours.html

Maps

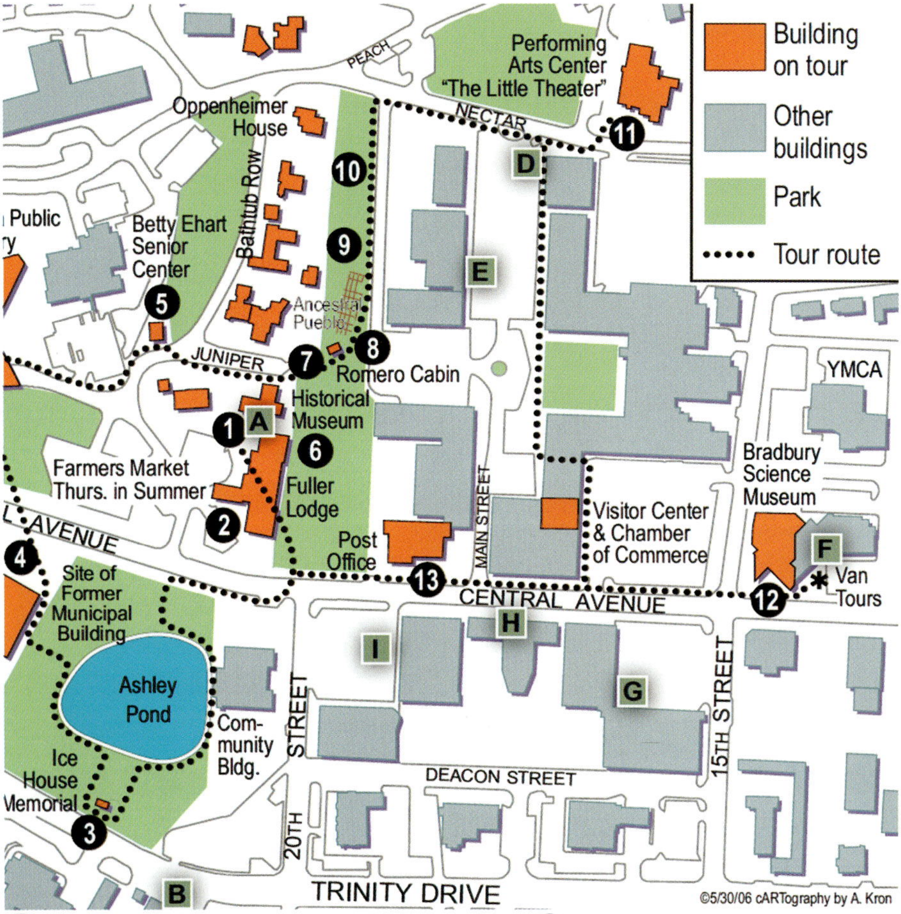

1. **Los Alamos Historical Museum & Book Shop**
2. **Fuller Lodge**
3. **Ice House Memorial**
4. **Site of Former Municipal Building**
5. **Betty Ehart Senior Center**
6. **The Los Alamos Memorial Rose Garden**
7. **Romero Cabin**
8. **The Big House Site**
9. **Ancestral Pueblo Dwelling**
10. **Bathtub Row**
11. **The Performing Arts Center**
12. **Bradbury Science Museum**
13. **Post Office**

Follow the dotted path to tour Los Alamos Manhattan Project Sites.
Map courtesy of the Los Alamos Historical Museum Archives